The Lake Effect

Sunset over the eastern bay of Lake Geneva, Wisconsin

The Joy of Lake Living

"Life is better on a lake."

- Robert M. Gullberg

~For all those lake lovers~

Printed in the United States of America. Acknowledgements: All images are free and not copyrighted. Front cover oil painting art: Caryl Anderson. Thanks to Jim Gullberg, Lin Barrett, John Gullberg and Laurie Stecher for editorial assistance.

Table of Contents

Why Read This Book?

You will enjoy reading this book whether you are curious about lakes or have already feasted on lake living. If you want to know more about how spending time around lakes provides an escape from the hustle and bustle and busyness of life, or a enchanting destination during a slow or ho-hum season of your life, read on!

Our planet is brimming with inland lakes that dot the landscape everywhere. There are an estimated 117 million of them spread throughout the seven continents – from pond-size to gigantic. For example, Alaska has about three million unnamed lakes, many considered too small to name, while the beautiful and mammoth Lake Baikal in Russia contains over one-fifth of the earth's fresh water supply!

With exception of Maryland, all 50 states are populated with at least one natural lake, with Alaska touting the most with over 3,000. Minnesota (with a license plate that claims "10,000 lakes") has the second highest total with about 15,291 natural lakes, most of them named, and Wisconsin has the third-highest number of lakes with 15,074, many of which are not. Michigan also has an abundance of lakes, totaling around 11,000.

There are so many beautiful lakes in the Midwest and beyond! But whether your favorite is Higgins Lake in Michigan, Lake Harriet in Minneapolis, Lake Ontario or one of the other five Great Lakes, the famed Lake Tahoe straddling Nevada and California, Lake Winnisquam in New Hampshire, the Finger Lakes in upstate New York, or Lake Mead in Arizona/Nevada, lakes carry a beauty and charm that engenders positive feelings and memories.

For the millions of lake enthusiasts out there as well as future lake enthusiasts, I hope you will relish this book. While the primary focus will be the beautiful Lake Geneva, nestled in the rolling hills and fertile farmland of southeastern Wisconsin, *The Lake Effect* is about the beauty and allure of lake living and all it has to offer. I will take you through the rich history of Lake Geneva and the treasure trove of beautiful memories it holds for me and my family who lived there for 26 years, and my hope is that it will trigger some beautiful memories of your own lake experience as well as some which may well be on your horizon.

Robert M. Gullberg

Dedication

This book is dedicated to my parents who ignited my love of lake living – Adrienne ("A") and Robert C. ("Bob") Gullberg. It was these city-dwellers from the North Side of Chicago who "saw the light" in the mid-1950's and were determined to make lake living a big part of their family's future. Without a doubt, growing up near the shores of Lake Michigan had a significant impact on their decision. In fact, I recall my Mom reminiscing about her parents taking her and her sister (Aunt Caryl) to Lake Michigan's great beaches for swimming and picnic lunches on many a sunny, summer afternoon.

Mom and Dad loved the sheer beauty of lakes. There was a mysterious magnetism about them, and they wanted to experience it together and with their family and to share it with others. They knew somehow deep down that spending time on a lake was settling for the soul. It enriched one's life and was life-giving. Growing up near Lake Michigan sparked their interest to explore smaller lakes further north after they married and moved inland to the northwest Chicago suburb of Park Ridge. Their lake search often took them into southern Wisconsin, where lakes are plentiful. Sunday afternoons would often involve my family picnicking, swimming, and playing on a Lake Geneva beach or public park, often in Williams Bay on the north central shore, or at the Riviera beach area on the east side of the lake. My earliest memories bring me back to wading in the cool shallows of Williams Bay and stepping on slippery rocks just offshore and throwing pebbles before I could even swim, at the tender age of three or four. It is there that the idea for this book started to take shape in my mind.

1   The Love Affair

Life is better on a lake! People all over the world can attest to this – whether they have grown up on or near one  or have vacationed on one for a day, week, month or more. It does not take much time on a lake to appreciate all it has to offer. When the lake beckons, there's a magnetic pull to experience the majestic; the sparkling water and waves, the sun and surrounding nature represents a perfect portrait and superb amphitheater of Creation. And the recreation it offers is second to none.

So whether young or old, wealthy or poor, urban, suburban, or rural, we feel a sense of invigorating refreshment around lakes. There is just something about them that feeds us to the depths of our souls. And those of us who have been fortunate enough to have experienced this marvelous effect share a common bond; the love affair with the lake we visit. We cannot seem to get enough of the special magic that a lake provides.

We had friends for many years who lived in a home on the western shores of Lake Michigan in Racine, Wisconsin. They would tell us, "There is nothing that compares to getting up in the morning and watching the ball of the sun come up at dawn or set in the early evening over the expansive lakeshore, whether it be summer or winter. It is so invigorating, it's almost a spiritual experience," they excitedly explained. That sentiment stands out to me to this day, and it certainly motivated my parents to find a place on a lake for their family to enjoy!

Our lives are about memories. In fact, I have heard it said that without memories, our lives lose their

meaning for us. I write this book with a plethora of recollections that have shaped my life and those of my siblings. That is what daydreaming is all about! For example, the photo above captures the Riviera public beach on the northeast end of Lake Geneva on a steamy hot, August afternoon. We spent many Sundays in our childhood enjoying this beach and the cheerful warmth of summer.

My brother Jim, sisters Lin and Laurie, and I were raised on this *captivating* lake. This sparkling blue lake is nestled in the rolling forested hills of the southeastern corner of Wisconsin. Our family lived on the southern shoreline of the eastern bay (called Geneva Bay) of this lake from 1966 to 1992.

What prompted me to write about Lake Geneva was

the cover of this book and what it means to me. My Mom's sister, Aunt Caryl, painted the view of the eastern Geneva Bay from our shoreline home, using this photo. What a spectacular view of the lake! The whitewashed pier, the green fiberglass Chris-Craft boat appropriately named "Abob", the avocado-colored striped canopy, the aluminum 12- foot fishing boat, and our Sunfish sailboat with the Swedish colors of blue and bright yellow are all in view. The photo captures the radiant sunlight on a warm, humid, July day. "Abob" was coined by my Mom--

Adrienne, who was often called "A" by my Dad, Bob. "Abob," of course, means to float.

Notice the bright yellow swimming raft anchored out from the pier about 50 yards. I can still "see it" bobbing up and down on a rough day on the lake, one in which "white caps" were in clear view. We spent many hours on that raft soaking in the sun, fraternizing with friends, and frolicking in the lake. The colors and reflections of the clear, silver-blue water, the wake of the speed boat skipping in the water in the middle of the bay, the small windsurfer on the left, and the larger sailboat in the distance lollygagging through the waves are reminders of the many activities that we experienced while living on this lake for 26 years.

There are two things to especially observe on the pier. Notice the lounge chair on the left-hand side of the pier. The pier was a favorite place for us to relax and turn a winter-faded chalky skin into a well-tanned bronze-colored complexion. Dad used to tan *so* easily, and though it is hard to tell, that is him in the picture.

Secondly, do you see the empty, wooden bench on the right side of the reverse "L" pier? It was on that bench that we spent endless hours over the years losing ourselves in conversation--catching up about life with family and friends. Most days it was a quiet place where you could hear nothing more than the small waves lapping against the pier posts. But other times, like a deer in headlights, we would find ourselves facing a menacing thunderstorm sneakily overtaking the lake's western sky (as seen in the photo on the right). It was amazing and

even exhilarating how quickly the dark clouds could eclipse a beautifully sunny sky to create an eerily dark scene. We would scamper up the hill to our house as soon as the wind whipped up!

I was the third of four children in my family, and fond memories of all of us hanging out at the lake are plastered in my mind. I have talked at length with my siblings about all our experiences there, and we love to share about all the nostalgic and magical memories that helped define our lives. My parents purchased our home there in the early 60's, when us kids ranged in age from six to 15, and we spent 26 years vacationing and visiting up there whenever we could, up until we were all in our 30's. But before I reminisce about our wonderful memories there, I would like to review the history and geography of this delightful lake –

its towns, and the surrounding area.

2

History of Geneva Lake

Lake Geneva (or Geneva Lake; it is called *both*) has a rich history. For centuries, the North American Indians made the shores around Geneva Lake their home. It is estimated that permanent Indian villages were established in southeastern Wisconsin around 900 A.D. At the same time across the Atlantic Ocean, the Vikings were thriving in Scandinavia.

For hundreds of years, Indians lived happily there, unimpeded by encroaching Europeans. French fur traders like explorer Jean Nicolet and Nicolas Perrot (see his

portrait on the left) came to the lake in the mid 1600's. It was 1673 when Marquette and Joliet explored along the Fox and Wisconsin Rivers, from Lake Michigan to the Mississippi.

Even by that time, there was evidence of Native Americans having lived there, likely for over a thousand years. Based on anthropologic findings, the ancient Oneota Tribes of the lost Hopewell Culture Indians had lived there. These agricultural peoples enjoyed an advanced civilization on Geneva shores as long ago as 1,000 B. C. They built effigy mounds in what is now Library Park, located in the city of Lake Geneva. Later, Ho Chunk, Menominee, Chippewa, Ottawa, and the Potawatomi Indians inhabited the Midwest, but it was primarily the Potawatomi tribe who called Geneva Lake home. They called it "Kishwau-ketoe Lake" (meaning 'clear water'.) The western shore of the lake (the present-day city of Fontana) is where Chief Maun-guh-zet (Big Foot) lived with his family in the early 1800's. About 60 or so families lived in their wigwams in that village. To this day, over 25 areas of Native Indian burial mounds have been found around the lake, but primarily on the northern shore in the Williams Bay region.

Today Big Foot Beach State Park on the eastern shore off Button's Bay carries the great chief's name. Occupying Lake Geneva's most eastern shores, it is unquestionably the best place to enjoy a lakeside sunset. Also, Ceylon Lagoon inside the camping and recreational park continues to be a local favorite for shoreline fishing in the area.

Gardens of melons, squash, onions, bean, corn, peas, and crops of tobacco flourished. Wild animals were described in abundance throughout the area: prairie wolves, raccoons, squirrels, foxes, otters, mink, and muskrats were plentiful. Frequent critter lake life included grouse, prairie chickens, quail, snipe, woodcock, plover, sandhill cranes, pigeons, partridge, wild geese, ducks, swan, loons, gulls, and pelicans. Fishing was (and still is) outstanding on the lake. Best catch included crappie, rock bass, bluegill, sunfish, perch, walleye, northern pike, lake trout, smallmouth bass, and largemouth bass.

It was in 1831 when "white man" John Kinzie and his party reached Geneva Lake and met with Big Foot (see his bronze sculpture on the right) at his village on the western shores. Kinzie and his party traveled between Fort Dearborn in Chicago and Fort Winnebago in Portage City,  Wisconsin. Subsequently, these later Indians were relocated by the United States Army to Kansas following the Black Hawk War of 1831-32. Treaty arrangements in 1833 laid the foundation for the eviction of Chief Big Foot

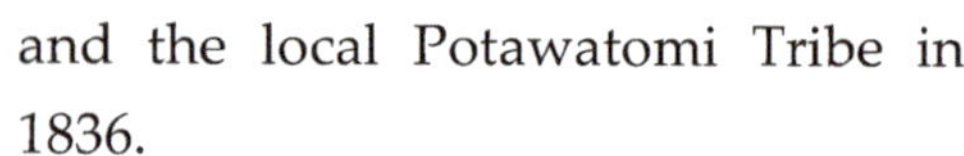

and the local Potawatomi Tribe in 1836.

John Brink (see his photo left), a government surveyor mapping the region, visited the lake later in 1834 and changed its name from Big Foot to Geneva Lake in honor of his hometown in Seneca, New York. He thought the area resembled the area of New York where he came from. Christopher Payne was the first recorded settler in the Village of Geneva and Walworth County in 1836.

By 1840, eight years before Wisconsin became a state, the Walworth County population containing Geneva Lake had mushroomed to 2,611. By 1850 it had blossomed to 17,862. The village of Geneva was incorporated in 1844. Other smaller lakes near Geneva were Lake Como and Lake Delavan, and the population around them also grew.

Located 90 miles northwest of Chicago, Geneva Lake become a magnet for city dwellers and Chicago suburbanites for well over 100 years. It is somewhat fortuitous how this happened. After the devastating Chicago fire in 1871, numerous wealthy families of Chicago made the 90-mile trip north to eventually build large estate mansions on the shores of the lake near the turn of the century.

Tracy C. Drake of the famed hotelier family (Drake Hotel in Chicago) gave renowned architect Howard Van Duran Shaw his first commission in Lake Geneva when he asked him to erect the Aloha Lodge on Lake Geneva's southern shore. Following the Lodge, in 1905, Adolphus Barlett, the founder of True-Value hardware tools and his wife Abbey commissioned Shaw to build what became as the 'House in the Woods.'

Business tycoons like P.K. Wrigley (1894-1977; see

photo left) of Wrigley Chewing Gum, Walden Shaw of the Yellow Cab Company, Gustavus Swift of the Swift Meat Packing, Ignaz Schwinn of the Schwinn Bicycle Company, the Charles Wacker family, as well as Wait Harris of the Harris Trust Company, were a few of many millionaire families who chose to build mansions to find some escape, rest, and recreation on the lake. In fact, Lake Geneva became known as the "Newport (Rhode Island) of the West." Prominent visitors in earlier years included Mary Todd Lincoln and Civil War Generals Sherman and Sheridan.

P.K. Wrigley's father (William Wrigley Jr.) purchased the Green Gables mansion of multimillionaire sportsman C.K.G. Billings in 1911. Black Point, on the southern shore, was a

Victorian mansion built for the Chicago beer baron (see photo previous page), Conrad Seipp in 1888. Black Point is especially significant because it was eventually acquired by the Wisconsin Historical Society and is open to the public today. It can be reached by excursion boat from the

Riviera docks on the northeast end of the lake. On the northeastern shore of Geneva Lake is Stone Manor, the largest mansion on the lake (see photo above) which was built by Chicago real estate entrepreneur Otto Young in 1903. Otto supposedly had this mansion built as a wedding gift to his daughter. Originally called "Younglands," it remains one of the most iconic and well-known landmarks on Lake Geneva.

These families saw the beauty of the lake back at the turn of the 19th-20th centuries, just like the Indians and others well before them. Though many years have come and gone, their estates continue to dot the shoreline landscape of the lake and can be easily viewed by boat. Excursion boat tours give tourists a rich sense of the history behind these dwellings and the families who inhabited them.

During the 1920s and throughout the early 30s, Lake Geneva enjoyed its share of gangster intrigue. Local rumors of tunnels that ran under buildings led to speculation of the area playing a large part in the Chicago-based bootlegger trade. Gangsters who profited from distributing illegal alcohol in the years of prohibition were well known to have escaped the city and FBI raids, sometimes fleeing to the far northern backwaters of Wisconsin.

One gangster, George 'Bugs' Moran (see photo right), was a local star player during prohibition days. Bugs often frequented nearby Lake Como (just a few miles north of Lake Geneva), bringing with him renowned bootleggers Baby Face Nelson and Jimmy Murray. At the  Lake Como Hotel, Bugs sought refuge and formed a friendship with one of the three brothers who owned the Inn. Herbert Hermansen, like most of Bug's cohorts, was not a fan of prohibition. He turned the basement of the hotel into a Speakeasy, stocking it with beer and nicknamed it the "Sewer." A speakeasy, also called a 'blind pig' or 'blind tiger', was an illicit establishment that sold alcoholic beverages. Speakeasies largely disappeared after Prohibition ended in 1933.

The history of Lake Geneva would not be complete without discussing Yerkes Observatory (see photo on the left), set on the shore of Williams Bay. It was built in 1892 to house the largest refractory telescope ever to observe outer space. The telescope's double lens was 40 inches in diameter. Yerkes is sometimes called the "birthplace of modern astrophysics," was the brainchild of astronomer George Ellery Hale, and financed by businessman Charles T. Yerkes. Hale coordinated the construction of the observatory with the University of Chicago. The 40-inch refractor was modernized in the late 1960's with newer electronics of the period. Yerkes stopped operation in 2018 but during its history collected 170,000 photographs. Notable astronomers who conducted past research at Yerkes include Edwin Hubble (who did his graduate work at Yerkes and for whom the Hubble Space Telescope was named), Dutch-American astronomer Gerard Kuiper (noted for theorizing the Kuiper belt, home to dwarf planet Pluto), and the 20th-century popularizer of astronomy Carl Sagan. Albert Einstein is also known to have visited the Yerkes Observatory (see his photo on the far left with a group of scientists) in May, 1921.

3   Geography of the Lake

On a clear and cloudless day, it was possible to see the 7 ½ miles from our pier across the 5,041-acre lake

expanse to the west side shore called Fontana. This picture is of seven year- old Amanda, my niece and oldest daughter of my sister Lin, posing on our pier on a rough day. Our large extended family loved spending lazy summer days together on the lake.

The width of the lake varies from about one-half to about 1.5 miles. Oblong in shape, it has a large appendage in the western-middle of the north shore named Williams Bay. We lived on the eastern end called Geneva Bay. Along with Fontana on the western end, these are the busiest hot spots for boating tourists. Three and four-foot waves at the "Narrows" in the middle of the lake were notoriously too rough for water skiing, but the wind would whip up making sailing there fantastic.

The distance around the lake is about 26 miles, and an unobstructed walking path along the shoreline

meanders around it. Native Indians (see photo above) used the trail long before the first Europeans. Early settlers decided to allow public access to the lake, and the 20 feet of land leading up to the shoreline is public domain." My siblings and I "walked the path" hundreds of times, mostly into the town of Lake Geneva to find things to do on hot summer days after swimming. Those walks along the path were always an adventure!

Like many lakes in southern Wisconsin, Lake Geneva was thought to have been formed by a receding glacier. Legend had it that there was an underground river that fed Lake Geneva, and that the deepest part of the lake was hard to find. Having said that, the depth at the "Narrows" is about 140 feet, with the average depth of the lake being 67 feet. The "Narrows" is simply the narrowest part of the lake seen below on the map and frequented by marathon swimmers, who like to swim across the lake in early mornings when the lake is still.

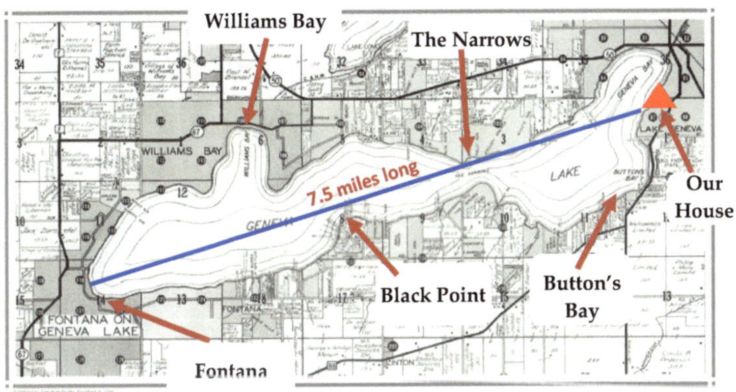

A map of the 7.5 mile-wide and oblong lake

The White River is a narrow river that flows out of Geneva Lake on the northeast end, wandering roughly 19 miles and then emptying into the Fox River in Burlington, Wisconsin. There, a dam of the Fox River in Burlington forms Echo Lake. White River zigzags through the small town of Lyons on its way to Burlington.

The remains of an 1800's dam is visible on Sheridan Springs Road where it crosses the river entering Lyons from the west. This formed a mill pond that is still shown on maps today even though it was drained several decades ago. White River floods often and is a popular canoe/kayak river in the region.

The Fox River (seen in the map below) travels approximately 139 miles south to Ottawa, Illinois where it joins the Illinois River. The Illinois River runs 112 miles to the west and north direction where it joins the Mississippi River. The green area in the map below shows the Fox River "watershed."

Part of the folklore of Lake Geneva has always been related to the clarity of its water. On calm, still mornings, the bottom of the lake can be seen up to fifteen feet. Being a relatively deep lake helps to keep it transparent like glass, and there is a good flow out of the lake via the White River, controlled by the Department of Natural Resources.

4 | The Town of Lake Geneva

Originally called "Maunk-suck" (Big Foot) for a Potawatomi chief, the city was later named Geneva in 1836 after the town of Geneva, New York, located on Seneca Lake, to which early settler John Brink saw a resemblance. To avoid confusion with the nearby town of Geneva, Illinois, it was renamed Lake Geneva.

The city of Lake Geneva is a quaint town located on the eastern shore of Geneva Lake. Just 10 miles north of the Illinois-Wisconsin border, it is a perfect destination for Milwaukeeans (45 miles northeast) and Chicagoans (80 miles south-southeast). The population has grown from around 5,000 in 1965 to 7,700 in 2020. The city is crawling with tourists in the summer months and shrinks back to its normal population in the fall, winter, and spring.

John Brink, a government surveyor, laid claim to the waterfall power and adjacent land on the east side of the lake at the White River outlet to the lake in 1835. In 1836, Christopher Payne, a pioneer settler from Belvidere, Illinois (just east of Rockford), built the first log cabin, the site of which is marked by a boulder and a plaque on Center Street just north of the river. Following a "Wild

West" battle to settle ownership, sawmills were built. Lake shore logs were floated to the mills and cut into lumber from which the town was built. Grain and flour mills followed. The fourteen-foot drop of water provided the most economical milling, and farmers brought their grain to Lake Geneva from as far away as Kenosha, Milwaukee, Belvidere, and Beloit. The town was surveyed and laid out in 1837.

Immigrants from New England soon flooded into the town. Most came via the Erie Canal and steamboat or sailing ships through the Great Lakes, embarking at Southport (Kenosha) or Milwaukee. By 1840, there were two hotels, two general stores, three churches, and a distillery added to the mills, cabins, and houses.

Railroads played an important role in the early growth of Lake Geneva, allowing it to develop into the distinguished resort destination it is today. Beginning in the late-1800s, wealthy Chicago families such as the Wrigley's (chewing gum), Maytag's (washers and dryers) and Schwinn's (bicycles) began enjoying visits. Prior to the railroad, the 83-mile trip could take a couple of

days. That began to change when the first train from Chicago, carrying 600 passengers, arrived on June 11, 1856, and was greeted with a celebration and marching band. By July of 1871, daily trains were in operation between Chicago and Lake Geneva via the Northwestern Railroad. The rail service provided a five-hour travel time outbound to Lake Geneva, with a shorter four-hour return to Chicago with fewer stops on the way back. The photo on the bottom of page 29 shows the Northwestern train at the Lake Geneva stop heading west to Williams Bay in 1965.

With the beauty of the lake and what it offered, families increasingly began building homes there, and the elaborate brick and stone exteriors were made possible through freight train service from Chicago and surrounding areas. With the original depot located at the intersection of Broad and North, the line was quickly extended to Williams Bay and the far west side of the lake in Fontana. From these depots, travelers set out for picnics and beach excursions, staying at country homes or at the area's first hotel, the Whiting House.

After the arrival of the railroad, thousands of tons of Lake Geneva ice were shipped each year to the Chicago market, until the beginning of World War II. Prior to refrigeration, ice was a "hot" commodity. Lake Geneva ice was prized for its clarity and quality, cut from the lake in large blocks, and was shipped via freight trains to be used in iceboxes back in Chicago.

Growth in demand and economic expansion also led to the development of several other rail lines, providing service to Lake Geneva and the surrounding area. By 1899, steam and electric railroads carried passengers from the Chicago suburbs to the west side of Lake Geneva in Fontana and brought in visitors from the Milwaukee suburbs. Total rail volumes continued to grow from 1899 through the end of World War II. By the 1950s however, automobiles, road building, and the expansion of the Interstate highway system drove a corresponding decline in rail traffic. The Williams Bay extension shut down in 1965, and the last train pulled into the Lake Geneva Depot in August 1975.

The iconic Riviera sits on its own large dock on the

lake in downtown Lake Geneva. It was erected by architect James Roy Allen in 1932. Originally, it was a big band music venue and dance hall with past performances by music celebrities the likes of Duke

Ellington, Ella Fitzgerald and Frank Sinatra. Those days were long gone by the time we moved to Lake Geneva in the mid 1960's. By that time, the Riviera served as a starting point for boat tours around the lake and as an arcade to buy popcorn, cotton candy, or play the pinball machines.

On the other side of the lake, the Abbey Resort

opened in Fontana in 1963 (see photo left). Named after European abbeys which gave rooms to weary travelers, the private investment group called Project Fontana purchased land on the western shore of Lake Geneva, and swamps were dredged to create the Abbey Marina and the 225-room hotel, the largest in the Midwest at the time.

In 1968, an ambitious young man from Chicago named Hugh Heffner opened his second Playboy Club (the first was in Chicago) just a few miles east of downtown Lake Geneva. The development included an airstrip, golf course, pools, fitness center and racquet club, and a lodge consisting of 350 rooms, a dance club, salon and three bar/restaurants. Staffed with women in the famed bunny apparel, the Lake Geneva Playboy Club hosted live performances by celebrities such as Bob Hope and Sonny and Cher. Guests of the Club could arrive by private plane onto the runway that lies at the tip of the ears of the bunny-shaped lake that Hefner had created on the property. In 1969, our family had dinner at one of its restaurants which was eye-opening, to say the least!

The quaint town of Lake Geneva nestled on the east side of the lake was always a fun place to visit. Its population of about 5,000 always increased dramatically during the gorgeous summer months because of tourist activity. It has been a popular destination for Chicagoans for over a hundred years because of all the lake offers, especially during the warm summer months.

Our favorite restaurant in downtown Lake Geneva

was Lake Aire, located on the southwest corner of Main and Broad Street. This mid-scale diner was perfect for our family and offered delicious burgers and fries.

For Sunday brunch, favorites were the Red Geranium restaurant on the east side of town on Hwy. 50, Interlaken, a resort on Como lake nearby just west of town, and Millie's Pancake Haus in Delevan. My parents hosted a big party for family and friends to celebrate their 25th anniversary there, and it was our family's very favorite restaurant.

5 | A Lake Geneva destination

How did our family end up at Lake Geneva? After all, there were numerous southeastern Wisconsin lakes within a short driving distance from the northwestern Chicago suburb of Park Ridge where we grew up: Fox, Powers, Grass, Paddock, Como, Delavan, Lauderdale, Beulah, Bohner, Hooker, Silver, Twin, Lauderdale, and Lily lakes to name a few. Like many opportunities in life, networking was the main reason we ended up at Lake Geneva.

Dad was many years into his dental practice at the age of 40 in Park Ridge, Illinois, one of the blossoming suburbs of Chicago post WWII when he got the "itch" to purchase a lake home. As if dentistry and raising a growing family to fill his time was not enough, Dad also obtained his real estate license and loved looking at lake and farmland property in southern Wisconsin.

One of his acquaintances was an orthodontist in Park Ridge who knew of Dad's interest in lake life and connected him to Dr. Neu, a fellow dentist who owned a beautiful home on the southeastern shores (off Hollybush Drive) of Lake Geneva, just west of Button's bay. Dr. Neu was recently widowed and was selling his home. On the Sunday we were visiting, it was a very windy day with frothy white caps. Despite the blustery weather, Dr. Neu was dead set on taking us out on the lake on his beautiful

20-foot inboard/outboard ski boat. Just as we got out on the lake, a storm quickly blew in and we had to exit the ride with haste. Dr. Neu had difficulty navigating the windy lake when he was parking and rammed the right rear of his boat into the pier, seriously damaging his boat. I remember the huge crack in the fiberglass.

Though the house was perfect for us, the price was too high for my Dad to accept. My Dad was always looking "for a deal," and I wonder if that storm might also have had something to do with his decision?! After all, the location on the bay would obviously pose a challenge to parking a boat on a windy day. So, my parents kept looking.

Our family spent several Sunday afternoons up at the public beaches of Lake Geneva when my siblings and I were quite young—especially on Williams Bay. I remember picnicking under a lone shade tree, no beach really, and walking along the slimy rockiness on the bottom of the lake in a foot of water. The other beach we frequented was in the town of Lake Geneva and adjacent to the Riviera pier, in front of the library. Wide and expansive (manmade), the beach was always packed with sun and lake worshippers. Our visits always included a large blanket on the beach with all the food and drink in the world packed in a picnic basket by Mom.

"Just looking" was a common theme for Mom and Dad when it came to real estate. They were looking for the right lake place at the right price. Never one to give up, Dad networked with O'Keefe Realty in downtown Lake Geneva. The taste of lake life was intoxicating, and they wanted it. O'Keefe showed them many places, and they often took us kids. They wanted us in on the action, and it was almost as if the venture was more for us than them. One place we looked at was on the north shore of eastern Geneva Bay. It was appealing, the price was right, but the house stood a full 300 feet above and off the lake, and the decline to the lake was at about a 30-degree angle. Mom and Dad thought about the rest of the extended family, and their advanced ages, and decided against the purchase.

The next place on Geneva that we looked at, we hit 'paydirt'. There was a small subdivision of smaller homes on the southeast shore of Geneva Bay that caught their eye. Betty Syver owned the property and built at least six houses on and near the lake in the early 1960s, and her son managed the properties. It must have been their shared Scandinavian heritage because Mom and Dad hit it off with Betty right away. The lake home at 11 Marianne Terrace "fit the bill." The home was handsomely landscaped and had a gentle hill sloping down to 101 feet of lake shore. It was a dream come true. After a 1-hour boat

ride on the son's 25-foot Mahogany wood and fiberglass Chris Craft ski boat (like the one in the photo on the left), Mom, Dad, and the four kids were sold. The price was right and in August 1966, "Bob-A-Links" was born.

Here is a photo of "Bob-A-Links" on the bottom left. Dad was "Bob", Mom was Adrienne ("A"), and the four

kids were the "Links". An avid bird lover, our grandmother "Mum" came up with the name. The black on white 'Bob-A-Links' sign hang freely on right side of the second story veranda for all to see. With his Swedish heritage, Dad was proud to have the blue and yellow national flag fly adjacent to the American flag off the veranda. This scene will be forever etched in our memories.

 6

Getting to the lake

The one hour and 15-minute commute to the lake from Park Ridge was mostly on Hwy. 12, winding through the northwestern suburbs of Chicago (Arlington Heights, Mt. Prospect, Palatine), then Lake Zurich past Bell Orchards, Volo, Fox Lake, Richmond, Genoa City, and finally Lake Geneva. By the time we got through Genoa City, we could feel the heady anticipation of arriving at 'Bob-A-Links', our destination. Our dog Tammy always accompanied us on our car trips and amazingly perked up when we were about five minutes away, jumping around in the back seat and trying to kiss my Dad's ear while he was driving, sensing we were getting close!

The sleepy town of Volo was a quick intersection in northern Illinois along the way. Besides the fact that it was a well-known "speed trap" for Chicago drivers, it had a

Ski and Sea Marine store where Dad bought our first ski-doo snowmobile (like the one seen in the photo here) in the winter of 1966-1967. Dad did not

waste much time getting into the business of having fun in the winter months on the lake. Along with the snowmobile, he purchased a sleigh-like attached sled that could be pulled behind the snowmobile so we all could experience the thrill of winter together.

The neighboring town of Fox Lake was known to us for two reasons. First, it was always a bottleneck for car traffic going through town, even in the 1960's. Highway 12 was only two lanes at the time. Second, and more importantly, it had a Dairy Queen! We always stopped for DQ, where Mom ordered her patented hot fudge sundae, Dad his chocolate ice cream cone so that he could drive with one hand, and the kids usually ordered cones or sundaes as well. There were a few small, sleepy hamlets several miles out of Fox Lake heading northwest—Spring Grove and then Solon Mills, just south of Richmond.

Richmond, Illinois, just south of the Wisconsin border was known for four things to us, and three were eating establishments. Orsolini's was a throwback

Italian family restaurant that we frequented for a quick dinner on the southeast corner of Hwy 12 and Hwy 31. The "Depot" was a trucker's breakfast diner where Dad loved to stop with us at 7 am in the morning for some tasty ham and eggs with hash browns and toast. These were the days of summer commuting for Dad from Lake Geneva to Park Ridge to keep his dental practice afloat. The third eating establishment was Dog 'N Suds (see photo left), the home of fast-food carports. It had the best hot dogs anywhere.

(Side note: Not the best of drivers -- and God rest her soul -- our great Aunt Jesse took a left turn out of there one day and almost got us all killed; a memory we will never forget!)

Finally, Ed Wendt's Boats was the place to purchase boats and fix ailing motors in Richmond. Dad knew the owner Ed well. We bought our fishing boat and yellow sunfish sailboat from him. We made many stops there over the years to have our beige and dependable Johnson 9.9 horsepower motor tuned up. Dad loved to look at new boats in Ed's showroom, and I remember the vinyl chemical smell of those new boats. Anytime I saw Ed, he was up to his elbows in grease fixing engines, and he smelled like gasoline.

Genoa City, Wisconsin was right over the Illinois border. It was indirectly made famous by Lee Phillip Bell in 1973- see her photo on the right. Lee was a long-time talk show host in Chicago at that time, and she commuted regularly to Lake Geneva. She and her husband created a famous CBS T.V. soap

opera called the "Young and the Restless," which 'on air' took place in Genoa City! Other than a corner movie theatre (that we sometimes attended) and an A&P grocery store, there was not much to it. In the 60's, it was pretty much a one-intersection town.

Once out of Genoa City, we traveled on the scenic two-laned Highway 12 curving through many densely packed corn fields as well as old farmhouses and finally arrived at the Badger High School intersection in Lake Geneva. Then we would pass the Lake Geneva Youth Camp, and head a short distance to Lake Shore Drive, which as the name implies, circles the lake. Our home on Marianne Terrace was a short distance from there and only a few homes down from the iconic Stone Manor.

When we arrived at "Bob-A-Links," a feeling of release and peace would settle in. Just getting out of the suburbs and traveling up to this lake oasis was a catharsis for our souls. It was a wonderful place of escape from the crazy rat race of suburban living.

7 # Summertime

The Midwest is blessed with some phenomenal summers, but us mid-landers know they are far too short! In southern Wisconsin, the last two weeks of May start to warm up, and by Memorial Day, it was time to party at 'Bob-A-Links.' For Mom, this always included an extended family party, from first cousins to second cousins once removed. It was not unusual to have over 20 or more family and friends gather for holidays or weekend visits.

Holiday parties were in the fabric of how our family lived. It started with Mum, my grandmother and Mom's mother and carried through to my Mom. Life enjoyment was always about parties on national holidays, and when there was not a holiday to celebrate, we created one!

Where there is a great party, there is great food, always prepared by Mom and Dad. Grilling burgers, brats, and hotdogs on the gas grill was my Dad's specialty.

While my Mom made endless lists and other preparations, it was Dad's 'duty' to travel to the nearby Sentry grocery store in downtown Lake Geneva to pick up the long list of food items—from buns, chips, beans, and salad dip, etc., to birthday cakes, ice cream, and of course Cruller's sweet rolls for the next morning's breakfast!

Memorial Day was usually the first holiday of the year we partied at the lake. Unfortunately, many Memorial Days were still a little chilly for swimming. Often, the summer did not start heating up until mid-June, and that marked the start of boating fun on the lake.

Dad was usually the captain of "Abob," our green, 20-foot Chris Craft ski boat. Over the years, the kids helped with taking the boats out on the lake. It was

our chore to keep the boat "spotless" as my Mom used to say. There was nothing that a wet rag soaked with lake water could not clean.

Our boat could handle four in the back seat, two in the front seat, and two or three others seated in the middle. Often, "Abob" was loaded to the gills with family and friends for hours of enjoyment. Boat rides on picture-perfect afternoons to the other end of the lake were our preferred way to spend hot summer days. On many of those two- hour trips, we would slow down inside the "Slow no Wake zone," and Mom and Dad would comment on the history of some of the scenic, historical mansions along the shore. For example, the mansion in the photo on the left was built in 1906 by Norman Harris, founder of

Harris Trust Bank. It is located on the northern shore of the lake close to the Narrows. In 1920, it was purchased by the Walden Shaw family who founded the Yellow Cab Company in Chicago. Finally, in 1998, it was bought by philanthropist Richard H. Driehaus.

"Boat rides" on the lake were part of our DNA. Dad probably captained hundreds of them over the years.

"Who is up for a boat ride," Mom would ask. Here we are sunbathing out on the lake on another gorgeous summer day.

Mom took great pleasure in "picnicking" on the lake with the family while we were growing up. We would take "Abob" halfway across the lake to the Narrows, stop the boat and take a leisurely swim, relax, and have a packed lunch. We lived for the warm sun and wind in our faces. "Abob" was a powerful in-board engine with its 185

horsepower that easily pulled water skiers and those that wanted to go inner tubing, such as my friend Edwin in the picture

here on the left. Sometimes we ventured all the way to

Fontana and visited the harbor of the Abbey lodge. It was also fun to motor under the bridge of S. Lakeshore Drive to see all the people enjoying the Fontana beach adjacent to Chuck's Bar, a well-known drinking establishment from about 1970.

Along the way, our 20-gallon gas tank on 'Abob' could be filled up at Button's Bay at VanDyke's, the Riviera pier, or at Gage Marina in Williams Bay. Unfortunately, gassing up on the lake was pricey because of the convenience it offered. We loved helping Dad gas up on these ventures, hopping up on the pier, keeping the boat stable and then shoving us off when finished. We enjoyed taking turns helping Dad captain the boat whenever possible.

The view of the lake is one of the joys we lived for-- a late, muggy, July afternoon looking out on an expansive

Geneva Bay was soothing to the soul. Having lots of family and friends on the pier taking in what the lake offered was also satisfying, because we loved sharing the lake with others. In the picture on the previous page, water

skiing and touring the lake is done for the day, as our Chris Craft has finally been hoisted out of the water, awaiting another day of fun.

The summer lake air had a sweet smell of its own too, produced by organic components from the seaweed in the lake. Once you have been intoxicated by this earthy fragrance, you never forget it. Similarly, the mildly musty odor in the basement of Bob-A-Links was ever-present in the summer months, and we loved it. Dad was sure to have the dehumidifier running continually all summer long to help prevent a flare-up of my Mom's summer allergies.

On Lake Geneva, the thousands of *piers* (not "docks," as there is no metal in them) that dot its shoreline are all painted bright white, and only white. That is how it has always been. Each year, piers are removed in the late fall, placed on the adjacent shoreline, and then each spring are put back in the lake. It was our responsibility as kids to paint the pier bright white and to give it a "lick and a promise" (i.e. brighten it up), like Mom used to say, every spring as soon as it was put in. Piers on the lake were made of heavy treated pine wood, but because of constant exposure to water, they would tend to slowly rot out, board by board, over a period of many years. Replacing this wood is a yearly, required religion, and our pier was no exception.

Our first summer at the lake was a sweltering one. In one stretch of weather, it was over 95 degrees for more than a week. There was no air conditioning in the house except for a small window unit in Mom and Dad's small second floor bedroom. As you would expect, all six of us slept in that bedroom to cool off for the week on various lounge cushions scattered all over the floor!

The mirror-like calmness of the lake at sunset seen in the photo below brought much peace at the end of a busy lake day, forever etched in our memories. The stillness on the lake could almost be deafening. Heavenly light

added a golden orange tint to the face of the lake, and it was paradise. It was the lake's way of rejuvenating after a busy day of boat traffic. Notice the huge oak tree on the right side of the picture. It had a perfect branch on which to hang a swing, but at 30 feet high, it was difficult initially to get the rope over the branch- we finally figured it out and enjoyed years of fun!

Sometimes we would go out on the pier between 11 pm and midnight. There was pitch black eeriness looking across the 7.5 miles of lake to the west of us. An occasional surfacing of a fish one or two hundred yards out in the middle of the lake made a distant splash. Even the flickering lights of water reflection from "town," as we called it, just east of us, was minimal.

As the summer heat would arrive in later June, so too would the boat/lake tourists, especially from Illinois. Tourism continues to be prevalent from Memorial Day to Labor Day when things finally cool off. Gage Marine has operated touring boats around the lake for decades. These large excursion vessels include Lady of the Lake (see

picture left), the Walworth, the Linn, and the Fontana. Tourists packed these boats daily for excursions around the perimeter of the lake, launching nearby from the Riviera pier. We loved jumping off the pier into the huge waves they made!

We were easily entertained as kids growing up on the lake. Just swimming off the pier doing our patented splash dives could keep us happy for hours. Even if you accidently got a gulp of water while diving or swimming, it tasted like a sweet medicine, a potion for our spirits. Sitting Bulls, cannon balls, jack knives, and Seven-Ups were the splash dives we worked to perfection. We were careful to grade each splash dive on a 1-10 scale. Dad always had the thickest cannonball splash, often scoring a "10," and Jimmy would get the biggest splash! My jack knife dives were also legendary.

While swimming, we could see millions of small Zebra snails mix with the muddy sand and inhabit the bottom of the lake. They generally left us alone. Occasionally, however, we would get "swimmer's itch" caused by these small gastropods. Over the years, chigger bites caused by shoreline Harvest mites were also occasionally encountered. When we did get bit, usually on our lower legs, we were in for a ferocious day or two of itching!

We also used to spend hours on the raft buoyed about  50 yards out from the pier on those balmy summer days and could literally talk the day away. Our neighbor friends Jeff, Sarah, and Sharon often joined us out there, along with other friends. The photo on the previous page shows sisters Lin and Laurie lolling around on it, having a long talk. Sometimes a few "scout" horseflies would find us, diving-bombing our shoulders or backs, leaving a painful bite to disrupt our peaceful visits. We also played "king of the raft" regularly and threw each other into the 15 feet of warm lake water with glee.

With all the swimming we did, we all became good swimmers. Once my brother Jim even swam across Geneva Bay over a mile on an early Sunday morning to Covenant Harbor, our church camp located directly across the bay. The lake was still with no waves, and his safety was monitored by us in our nearby fishing boat.

Since we were from a Chicago suburb, we were long-time Cubs fans. Every afternoon when the Cubs games were broadcast on the radio, we had WGN blasting on the pier. That was the era of Ernie Banks, Ron Santo and Billy Williams, and radio play-by-play was by the famous Lou Boudreau and Lloyd Petit. We loved it!

The dog days of summer could be long, despite all the opportunities for fishing, swimming, sailing, and waterskiing. One of the fun things we liked to do was stroll along the shoreline

The shoreline path around Lake Geneva

path into town. It was about a 30- minute walk, and during the walks, we would pass through forested property and by a few huge mansion homes with pristine landscaping as well. The Stone Manor was a few piers down from us - a Victorian mansion built at the turn of the 20th century, and they had guard dog German Shepherds that scared us to the core. We would sprint past their property in the hopes of not encountering them! Upon arriving at the "packed-to-the-gills" tourist town, we shopped for candy, slipping in and out of the penny arcades, and licked big, colorful snow cones.

Sometimes in the early mornings, we cruised our light aluminum three-seated fishing boat (which could get up to about 22 M.P.H) and zoom over to the small harbor near the town of Lake Geneva. We ventured back into a small inlet of the lake where the White River started in its trek to meander into the Fox River. To do this, we had to go under the bridge of Broad Street (renamed Wrigley Drive.) This is the very boat that I used when I taught my little sister Laurie how to slalom ski.

Whenever they could steal the chance, teenagers Laurie and first cousin Jan would sneak out in the darkness of night and "skinny dip" off our pier, sitting on an innertube out on the water. Somehow, they pulled this off without others knowing!

We had a lot of fun frolicking on innertubes on the lake during the day. They were slippery as could be. We would always select the perfect spare truck innertube from the gas station in town. We would play on them out on the water, and later we started pulling riders on it behind our ski boat long before "tubing" was popular.

On rainy days, we played a lot of games like Monopoly and card games like Uno, and we also loved to watch the Cubs on TV. The late 70's was the era of a professional tennis player and Swede named Bjorn Borg. We loved to watch him play, and he ignited a love for tennis. We would also sometimes head over to the nearby Badger High School and play tennis in the sweltering heat of late July or August on their deserted courts. We also like to go for runs around the high school which culminated in a dip in the lake. We always found fun things to do!

Sailing

The thrill of the wind on a blustery day on the lake got us excited about sailing aboard our yellow Sunfish back and forth across the large Geneva bay. Sometimes, we ventured further—all the way to the Narrows. There was nothing quite like a fully extended sail flying with the wind riding the white-capped waves! We all loved to sail. The rush of it all, just hearing the wind in our ears, seeing the seagulls circling and swooping, and the waves lapping against the bottom of the boat! The up and down glide on our sunfish over four-foot waves was better than any carnival ride.

Summer Sunday regattas were a regular beautiful spectacle. Larger boats with their spinnakers took a lot of skill to maneuver, as in the photo below, especially in competitive races. Dad later invested in a Boston Whaler, but we never truly mastered it.

We were perfectly content with the sunfish to play around with. The photo on the next page shows Laurie,

Bobby, and Lin coming in from a nice afternoon sail across the lake. Wearing white "buoy belts" for safety was a law.

Waterskiing

Skiing on the surface of a lake gave us a feeling that is difficult to put into words. There is a 'high' with waterskiing when you are skidding over the water with the thick churns of water splashing on you with every turn. The word "magical" comes to mind. Whenever there was a calm day, we could not wait to get out there to experience it.

Waterskiing was the first sport we all tried to master when we got our place at the lake. It is a sport that takes a lot of time and effort to master. The exhilaration of gliding across the water at 25 M.P.H. really gets the heart pounding. Dad had previously water-skied up at White

Sand Lake in Lac de Flambeau, northern Wisconsin in the summers of 1961-1965.

Jim, Lin, and Bobby started skiing the first summer. Jim and Bob skied slalom and always 'hot-dogged' from the get-go, jumping the boat waves with reckless abandon. Fortunately, there were no accidents, except when our next-door neighbor's fiancé got up out of the water not knowing that her bikini top had fallen off!

Laurie, at the age of seven, was waterskiing behind our aluminum 12-feet long fishing boat, being pulled by a 9.9 horsepower Johnson outboard motor. She made it look easy and graduated to adult skis quickly especially once she learned to slalom, though the Acapulco wooden skies were twice as high as she was!

Our favorite skiing times were early in the morning  before other boats were on the lake, when the lake was "like glass-" monastery quiet. We also looked for times right after dinner before the sun went down. Though we probably were not aware of it at the time, the memory of these idyllic scenes on the lake will take our breath away forever. The photo above captures one of the author's favorite memories of years gone by.

Button's Bay always had the smoothest water for stress-free skiing, along with a cove-like area just east of the Lake Geneva Country Club on the south shore of the lake. We rarely went west of the Narrows for more places to water ski. The only places my sisters did not like to ski were in the areas along the shore with high weeds where the big fish roamed.

Many of our friends who ventured up on weekends wanted to learn how to waterski. It took a lot of patience for the boat driver! A big challenge was dealing with boat traffic during peak times. Ski boats produced random and unpredictable large waves that spelled doom for the skier. It also made it hard for the skier to get out of the water. Dropping a ski, from two to one, though done on some less busy lakes, was not allowed on Lake Geneva because of safety issues and Dad did not allow this stunt from the beginning. Once a skier fell, the driver of "Abob" always circled back quickly to pick up the skier, and the skier would hold a ski straight up in the air so boaters could see them.

Fishing

As a fishery, Lake Geneva is naturally teaming with a multitude of midwestern game fish. The Department of Natural Resources stocks it regularly. Just off the shore in 2-10 feet of water all around the lake are panfish such as the orange-eyed rock bass, the multi-colored bluegill, the mandarin-colored sunfish, perch, and crappie. These can be caught with anything from a piece of cheese to a quarter of a nightcrawler worm. Smallmouth bass are teaming in waters between 6 and 25 feet. Walleye, northern pike, and even an occasional largemouth bass, lake trout, or musky are lurking in the deeper waters or weedier areas of the lake. It takes some work to find these game fish.

Fishing on the lake was always a delight. Lake Geneva is a fisherman's paradise. In the photo on right, my cousin Jill is learning how to fish with  my help off the pier. Because of the 100's of piers dotting the shoreline, there are large "cribs" of heavy rocks under the water that hold them in place. "Cribs" are wooden structures filled with boulders found under the piers. They house thousands of fish and support a great habitat for blue gills, rock bass, sun fish, perch, smallmouth and largemouth bass. Any one of these fish can be caught on pretty much every cast in the shallows by the shore out to 10-feet deep. We grew up casting bobbers and worms into the shallow water of 2-5 feet deep. We were sure to get our share of blue gills there, very ripe for the taking. Pound for pound, there is nothing like the fight of a fat bluegill!

We loved the preparation for fishing the next day by catching "night crawlers". Brother Jim and I would water the top level of grass for about 2-3 hours, and then at night after 10 PM, we would go out with our flashlights and coffee can filled with fresh, black dirt. We would catch dozens of juicy worms in an hour or so. You had to be fast though to pinch them. They would dive under the ground in a split second. Being still and quiet was the key, and the lights from the flashlights did not bother them.

I often casted for smallmouth bass with surface lures such as a Hula popper which easily disturbed their sleep. You knew when a smallmouth bass hit the popper because as soon as they were snagged, they would jump out of the water several times. My favorite place for smallmouth was right near the Stone Manor pier, which was an ideal environment for them and many other fish, especially with all the rock beds around. Their pier was quite long!

Before they were outlawed, soft shelled crabs were used to catch bass, and smallies loved them. Our neighbor frequently fished with crabs and boasted of their ability to attract smallmouths. Another favorite place of mine for bass was out in front of the Riviera pier, where there was a 6-8 feet sand bar going 100-150 yards out into the lake.

For fat rock bass, we casted small Mepp's spinners in water between 4-10 feet. They hit the lure hard. Trolling with a spinner behind the boat drives the rock bass crazy in 10-15 feet of water.

Walleye fishing was always tricky, but Geneva Bay was a factory for these good-eating fish. Just past the sandbar out from the Riviera dock and the Covenant Harbor featured a great natural habitat for walleye in 15-25 feet of water. Artificial deep diver lures such as Cisco's would murder them, or minnows after nightfall.

Northern pike would occasionally be caught in 30-40 feet of water of the Maytag estate point, or out in front of the Lake Geneva Country Club while fishing with artificial Red-eyes, dare devils, or 6-inch suckers. They will bite just about anything, and with their sharp teeth, you had to be prepared with leather gloves to de-hook them.

One of the fun ways to catch bullhead was to throw a 6-inch perch out at night off our pier hooked behind the dorsal fin. We caught some nice three-five-pound bullhead doing that. Every lake has scavenger fish, and Geneva is no different. The ugly garfish and carp fish can also be found there. We used to scare our sisters and friends to death with the sheer mention of them swimming anywhere near our pier!

On one rough and windy day on a mid-morning Saturday, Jim and I went out a hundred yards from the pier fishing. In the glistening sun, suddenly I spotted something large flailing in about six to seven feet of water off the community pier, just a few of piers over. Jimmy yelled, "That's a kid in trouble!" We hot-tailed over there, indeed it was a nine-year-old boy who obviously could not swim well, and his purple blue body was in the process of drowning. He happened to be deaf and mute, so communication was difficult. Jim quickly jumped in and brought the kid to safety of the shoreline and turned him over so water in his lungs would come out, and he could be resuscitated. Over the next 15 minutes, his purple skin slowly warmed up, and he came alive! That was an event that we will never forget. His Mom will be forever thankful to Jimmy for saving her boy's life!

Golf Nearby

Summer golf was always an afternoon getaway, nine or 18 holes, - it did not matter. We frequented the courses around the lake, but most commonly Hillmoor Golf Club, right on Highway 50 heading out of town on the east end. It had scenic rolling hills with pin-point sized greens and just a few sand traps to keep the pace of play up.

Other courses were played less frequently but included Abbey Springs (in Fontana), Country Club Estates, George Williams College course (near Williams Bay), and sometimes we would drive down to Richmond, Illinois just over the border and play Hunter Country Club. Golf was usually a family affair for the guys.

We'll never forget our brother-in-law Cliff's hole-in-one on the short par 3- 115 yard hole #10 at Hillmoor Golf Club, or him holing out from 120 yards for a score of 5 on the long par 5- 16th hole on the back nine on a sweltering hot, sunny afternoon August day. He was an infrequent golfer, so his feats were that much more memorable, and we had a lot of fun celebrating after the round.

Indoor Fun

Nights and days on the lake were filled with years of laughter. There were no computers, video games, or social media to keep us preoccupied! In this way, the 1960s and the early 70's was good for family life. Mom and Dad played a lot of the game Bridge with Aunt Caryl and Uncle Donn when they visited every summer. When our friends visited, we played Spades, Hearts, Uno, or Yahtzee with an occasional game of Monopoly thrown in. We especially liked playing these games during long thunderstorms in the summer or during the cold winter months. Dad prided himself on building cozy fires in our natural wood fireplace which burned long on those winter weekends. Hot chocolate was always made ready for us by Mom after long hours playing in the snow- tobogganing, ice skating on the lake and snowmobiling. Those were some fun winter days!!

 8 # Off Season- Spring and Fall

Springtime was the season when our lake thawed, and the grass turned from brown to green. We did not get up to the lake from Chicagoland much from March to near the end of May, especially since we were busy with school. We waited with great anticipation for summer to come.

Trees started changing to their fiery colors beginning on Labor Day, the first weekend of September. The lake water chilled, and any water skiing would require a wet suit, which we used in later years. Come Halloween-time, the pier had to be pulled out with large winches onto the lakeshore to sleep for another frosty winter. Fall was a special time at the lake, with the changing and falling of the leaves and their crunch under our feet. As the memories come flooding back, I can still smell, hear, and feel them as though it was yesterday. We sure had our share of raking to do with our towering oak tree and giant sugar maples which dominated our landscape down to the shoreline. Oh, were their colors vibrant! What a sight to behold with their crimson colors reflected on the water. Fall at the lake was a beautiful and reflective time. Everything was quiet; the lake became deserted, as boats were pulled off the lake by Gage Marine and stored until the following Spring.

The above picture in front of Covenant Harbor captures the beauty of Lake Geneva in the fall. A chill is in the air and it is almost time to retire the boats and wooden piers from the lake.

<table><tr><td>9</td><td></td></tr></table>

Winter

Winter in Lake Geneva had a beauty and charm all its own but drastically different than summertime. The Chicago area and Milwaukee tourists were gone. The streets were empty and there were no traffic jams. It was blustery and cold, especially in January and February, typical of Midwest winters. It was peaceful to be sure, but it also made you long for the warm and balmy summer to return. Our family went up to the lake less frequently during winter but enjoyed what it had to offer.

The Lake Geneva Public Library on Main Street holds special memories. Dad was on the Board there in the late 80's and early 90's. He loved to read, particularly historical biographies and suspenseful fiction. I studied there periodically while attending medical school, gazing out on the wide and expansive ice covering the lake, daydreaming about summer. How different the lake looked in the winter months!

Wintertime on the lake was a wonderland. Sometimes Geneva Bay would freeze like a plate of glass, and we would have our own 300-yard skating rink right out from our front lawn. Next door was a great hill for tobogganing down to the lake, and we loved to see how

far we could get out on the lake with each run. We were so busy having fun in the frigid air that we did not even think about the cold until we got inside for our proverbial mug of hot chocolate. Uncle Ray (our step-grandfather as seen in the photo above with Lin and Laurie) was in his late seventies when he would trudge out in the snow and watch us ice skate on the lake or play a pick-up game of hockey. When the lake froze like a plate of glass, the ice was transparent, and you could see the bottom of the lake up to 15 feet or so. At dusk, I remember it being peaceful and as still as a tomb out on the lake.

The first thing Dad did when he bought Bob-A-Links was to erect a flagpole by the lake (see his photo on the top of the next page). The son of Swedish immigrants, he had an abiding respect for our country and wanted others to as well. In the photo, he is with our dog Tammy waving to us on a crisp winter day. Notice the numerous ice "shanties"

dotting the northern bay landscape. Though we did not ice fish ourselves, hundreds of people braved the arctic temperatures in their small homes on the lake and would drive right up to them in their cars. That's how thick the ice was!

On most winter days, we went from tobogganing to ice skiing to riding our snowmobile. Our yellow and black striped ski doo snowmobile was one of the originals purchased at the Munson Marine in Volo, Illinois. It only topped out at about 40 M.P.H. but was still a blast. Dad used to love to explore the shoreline with it at night. Tammy, our medium-size, blue-grey-haired Kerry Blue Terrier, was driven nuts by the snowmobile and chased it incessantly. I remember slamming into a tree once or twice while riding it, but fortunately, no injuries! Back in those days, helmets were never worn. Unfortunately, head safety was the furthest thing from our minds. It is a miracle we all survived without any serious injuries.

Ice boating was a sport that we loved to watch, but we did not get to see these peculiar boats on the lake often. When the lake froze like a plate of glass, we saw wooden ice boats--basically a hull attached a perpendicular cross piece with three skates—one in the front and two on the sides in the back-- darting across the lake. Ice boats need relatively snow-free ice to sail and are usually built for only one person. They can travel well over 60 M.P.H. and you could hear an ice boat a mile or two away because of the hum and vibration it makes as its skates cut into the ice.

Wintertime walks on the lake path were invigorating but sometimes difficult because of all the ice and snow, sometimes two or three feet high on the bank around the lake. But it never stopped us from exploring and experiencing the beauty of winter up at the lake.

Conclusion

The joy and wonder of lake living will be imprinted in my mind forever. Lake Geneva has done that for me. I realize how fortunate I am to have been given the opportunity to experience it, and I will always be grateful. For those of you who have spent much time around a lake or have a permanent residence on one—anywhere-- well, you are indeed blessed as well. And just as Lake Geneva has written these memories on my heart, your lake experiences have written their own story for you. The spirit and beauty of lakes can capture your imagination regardless of how and where you experience them. It is my sincere hope that the power of this earthly creation will captivate you as much as it has me.

Bibliography

1. Annals of Lake Geneva, 1835-1897, by James Simmons.
2. History of Walworth County, 1882.
3. History and Indian Remains of Lake Geneva and Lake Como, Walworth County, Wisconsin. 1930. Jenkins.
4. The Book of Lake Geneva. Chicago, Illinois; Chicago Historical Society in collaboration with the University of Chicago Press, 1922.
5. Discover Lake Geneva: A Guide to the Historic Lakefront Homes. Williams Bay; Wis: Gage Marine, Inc., 2003.
6. Fogle, Phil. Grassroots-Lake Geneva. Wi: Big Foot Publishing Company, 1986.
7. Geneva Lake, by Carolyn Hope Smeltzer and Martha Kiefer Cucco, 2014
8. Lake Geneva: Life at the Water's Edge by Michael Keefe (2006)
9. Multiple internet sources, including: https://worldpopulationreview.com/state-rankings/states-with-the-most-lakes).